Modern Job Alchemy

Transforming Challenges into Opportunities in Today's Employment Arena

Written by

Morgan E. Blake

Independently published

2024

Introduction: The New Alchemy of Employment

Embracing Change in the Job Market

In the ever-evolving tapestry of the job market, **embracing change** is not merely a choice but a necessity for those aspiring to thrive. As we delve into the intricacies of this transformation, it's imperative to understand that the job market of today bears little resemblance to its predecessor. The digital revolution, a surge in globalization, and the unforeseen challenges posed by global events have collectively rewritten the rulebook of employment.

The advent of technology has been a double-edged sword; while it has made some jobs obsolete, it has also birthed new industries and opportunities. The rise of artificial intelligence, machine learning, and automation has reshaped the skills landscape, demanding a workforce that is not only tech-savvy but also adaptable and continuously learning. The gig economy, once a mere footnote in the employment sector, has burgeoned, offering flexibility and autonomy but also presenting challenges in job security and benefits.

To truly **embrace change** in this dynamic environment, one must adopt a mindset of perpetual growth and learning. The first step in this journey is recognizing the transient nature of job roles and industries. What was considered a stable career path a decade ago may now be on the brink of transformation. This realization should not be a source of trepidation but rather a beacon guiding us towards adaptability and resilience.

Adaptability, in this context, involves a willingness to acquire new skills and competencies, to pivot when necessary, and to view change as an opportunity rather than a threat. It's about looking beyond traditional employment paradigms and being open to unconventional career paths, be it in the burgeoning fields of renewable energy, digital marketing, or cybersecurity.

Resilience, on the other hand, is about maintaining a steadfast commitment to one's career objectives amidst the whirlwind of change. It's about building a robust professional network, nurturing soft skills such as communication, leadership, and emotional intelligence, and maintaining a positive outlook even when the path ahead seems uncertain.

Furthermore, the modern job seeker must become a master of personal branding. In a world where digital presence is as significant as physical presence, curating an online persona that reflects one's professional capabilities, achievements, and potential is crucial. This involves not just maintaining an up-to-date LinkedIn profile but also engaging with industry communities, contributing to professional forums, and showcasing expertise through various digital platforms.

In embracing change, one must also recognize the importance of **continuous learning**. The concept of education being confined to the early years of one's life is outdated. The modern professional is a lifelong learner, constantly updating their skill set through online courses, workshops, and certifications. This commitment to learning not only enhances employability but also enriches personal development, opening doors to opportunities that were previously inconceivable.

As we navigate through the modern job alchemy, it's essential to remember that change is the only constant. The ability to adapt, to learn, and to remain resilient in the face of change is what will define success in this new employment arena. It is in this spirit that we embark on this journey together, transforming challenges into opportunities and paving the way for a fulfilling and prosperous career path.

The Philosophy Behind Modern Job Alchemy

At the heart of **Modern Job Alchemy** lies a philosophy deeply rooted in the belief that within every challenge lies a hidden opportunity waiting to be unearthed. This guiding principle shapes our approach to navigating the labyrinth of the modern job market, transforming perceived obstacles into stepping stones towards fulfilling careers. It's a mindset that doesn't just adapt to change; it embraces it, harnesses it, and turns it into a powerful ally.

Adaptability, **Innovation**, and **Resilience** form the triad of core tenets underpinning this philosophy. Together, they forge a path through the complexities of contemporary employment, guiding individuals towards not just surviving but thriving in an ever-evolving landscape.

Adaptability is the first pillar, emphasizing the importance of flexibility and openness to new experiences. In a world where change is the only constant, the ability to pivot and embrace new directions is invaluable. It's about viewing change not as a daunting upheaval but as a series of opportunities to grow, learn, and evolve. This mindset encourages us to continuously reassess our skills and goals in light of the shifting job market dynamics, ensuring we remain relevant and competitive.

Innovation stands as the second pillar, driving us to think creatively and outside the conventional paradigms. It's the spark that ignites new ideas, propelling us forward into uncharted territories. In the context of job alchemy, innovation is about reimagining our career paths, exploring unconventional roles, and applying our skills in novel ways. It's about seeing beyond traditional job titles and industry boundaries, finding niches where our unique talents can shine.

Resilience, the third pillar, is our bedrock, providing the strength and perseverance needed to navigate the ups and downs of career development. It's about cultivating a robust inner fortitude that enables us to face setbacks and challenges without losing sight of our goals. Resilience is what keeps us moving forward, even when the path is uncertain, fueling our determination to overcome obstacles and emerge stronger on the other side.

The philosophy of Modern Job Alchemy also embraces the concept of **lifelong learning** as a critical component of career success. In an age where knowledge and skills can quickly become outdated, the commitment to continuous education and self-improvement is essential. It's about fostering a curious mind and a thirst for knowledge, ensuring we remain at the forefront of industry trends and innovations.

Personal branding and **networking** are also integral to this philosophy, highlighting the importance of how we present ourselves and connect with others in the professional realm. A strong personal brand communicates our value proposition, while an extensive network provides support, opportunities, and insights.

In essence, the philosophy behind Modern Job Alchemy is a call to action, urging us to view our careers as a dynamic journey rather than a static destination. It's about embracing the fluidity of the job market, leveraging our strengths, and continually seeking ways to add value in our chosen fields. It's a reminder that, with the right mindset and strategies, we can transform the challenges of today's employment landscape into opportunities for growth, fulfillment, and success.

Chapter 1: Understanding the Modern Job Market

Evolution of Employment: From Industrial to Digital

Tracing the evolution of employment from the industrial era to the digital age unveils a remarkable journey, one marked by profound shifts in the way we work, the nature of our jobs, and the skills we require to thrive. This transformation is not merely a change in technological tools or workplace environments; it represents a fundamental redefinition of employment itself, reshaping our societal structures, economic models, and individual career trajectories.

The Industrial Age: A Look Back

The industrial revolution, spanning from the late 18th century into the early 20th century, marked the beginning of this evolution. It was a period characterized by the transition from agrarian societies to industrial powerhouses, where manual labor was gradually replaced by machinery. Factories became the epicenters of production, and the workforce shifted en masse from farms to manufacturing hubs. Employment during this era was defined by routine, manual tasks, with workers spending long hours in factories under often harsh conditions.

As we progressed through the industrial age, advancements in technology, transportation, and communication began to lay the groundwork for the next significant shift—the transition to a service-based economy. The mid-20th century saw a boom in sectors like healthcare, education, and retail, signaling a move away from manufacturing-centric employment.

The Advent of the Digital Age

The late 20th century heralded the onset of the digital age, driven by rapid advancements in computing power, digital technology, and the internet. This era has transformed every aspect of employment, from the creation of entirely new job categories to the demise of others, from the way we search for jobs to how we perform them, and even where we work.

In the digital age, information and knowledge have become the new currency, with **data literacy** and **digital fluency** emerging as critical skills. Jobs that were once manual and task-specific have evolved into roles requiring analytical thinking, problem-solving, and adaptability. The rise of **automation** and **artificial intelligence** has further accelerated this shift, automating routine tasks and pushing the workforce towards more complex, creative, and strategic roles.

The Gig Economy and Remote Work

Another hallmark of the digital age is the rise of the gig economy. Platforms like Uber, Airbnb, and Freelancer have created ecosystems where short-term contracts or freelance work are the norms, not the exception. This shift towards project-based, flexible work arrangements has redefined the traditional employer-employee relationship, offering unprecedented freedom and flexibility but also raising questions about job security and benefits.

Parallelly, technology has made remote work not just feasible but highly efficient, breaking down geographical barriers and opening up global opportunities. The recent global events, particularly the COVID-19 pandemic, have acted as a catalyst, demonstrating that many jobs can be done effectively from anywhere, challenging long-held notions about office-centric work cultures.

The Skills Revolution

As we navigate through the digital age, the demand for **new skills** is incessant. Digital literacy, coding, digital marketing, and data analysis are just the tip of the iceberg. Soft skills like emotional intelligence, critical thinking, and adaptability have become equally important, as they are the hardest to automate and the most crucial in a rapidly changing job landscape.

Embracing Continuous Learning

The relentless pace of change in the digital age necessitates a culture of **continuous learning** and personal development. The concept of a job for life has become outdated, replaced by a model of lifelong learning and career adaptability. Professionals are now expected to continuously update their skills, whether through formal education, online courses, or self-directed learning, to remain relevant in their fields.

Conclusion

The evolution from industrial to digital employment is a testament to human ingenuity and adaptability. It reflects our capacity to innovate, to redefine our societal structures, and to continually adapt to new challenges and opportunities. As we look towards the future, it's clear that the journey of employment evolution is far from over. The digital age is set to continue transforming the job market, demanding flexibility, creativity, and a lifelong commitment to learning from all of us in the workforce.

Key Trends Shaping Today's Job Landscape

As we navigate through the complexities of the modern job market, it's crucial to understand the key trends that are shaping our employment landscape. These trends are not just fleeting changes; they represent significant shifts in how we work, where we work, and the skills that are in demand. By grasping these trends, we can better prepare ourselves for the opportunities and challenges that lie ahead.

The Rise of Remote Work

One of the most profound changes in recent years has been the dramatic rise of remote work. Fueled by advances in technology and, more recently, by the necessity brought about by global health challenges, companies across the globe have adopted remote working models at an unprecedented scale. This shift has not only changed where we work but also how organizations manage their workforce, prioritize tasks, and measure productivity. Remote work has opened up a world of possibilities for job seekers, allowing for greater flexibility and access to opportunities far beyond local job markets.

The Gig Economy and Freelancing

The gig economy continues to grow, reshaping the traditional employer-employee relationship. More individuals are now opting for freelance work, attracted by the promise of flexibility, autonomy, and the ability to choose projects that match their skills and interests. This trend towards project-based, short-term contracts is altering the career trajectories of many professionals and requires a different approach to career stability, benefits, and long-term planning.

Technological Advancement and Automation

Technological advancements, particularly in automation and artificial intelligence (AI), are transforming the job market. While some roles are being automated, new ones are emerging that require a new set of skills. Jobs that remain are evolving, as AI and machine learning tools augment human capabilities. Staying ahead in this environment means continuously updating one's skill set to include digital literacy, data analysis, and an understanding of emerging technologies.

The Importance of Soft Skills

Despite the rise of automation, soft skills remain irreplaceable and are becoming increasingly important. Skills such as emotional intelligence, critical thinking, creativity, and adaptability are highly valued by employers across industries. These skills enable professionals to navigate complex work environments, lead effectively, and foster innovation. As technical skills can become outdated quickly, soft skills provide a foundation for continuous learning and adaptation.

Sustainability and Social Responsibility

There's a growing trend towards sustainability and social responsibility in the business world. Companies are being held accountable for their impact on the environment and society, leading to an increase in jobs related to sustainability, corporate social responsibility (CSR), and ethical business practices. Professionals with knowledge in these areas, as well as those who can integrate sustainability into various roles, are in high demand.

Lifelong Learning and Continuous Education

The concept of lifelong learning has never been more relevant. The rapid pace of change in technology and business models means that what we learn today may need to be updated or expanded tomorrow. Professionals must commit to continuous education, whether through formal degrees, online courses, or self-directed learning, to remain relevant in their fields.

Personal Branding and Digital Presence

In a world where the first point of contact is often digital, personal branding and a strong online presence have become essential. Professionals must be able to effectively communicate their skills, experiences, and values online, leveraging platforms like LinkedIn, personal websites, and social media to network and showcase their expertise.

Globalization and Diversity

The global nature of business today means that companies are looking for professionals who can work effectively across cultures and geographies. Diversity in the workforce is not just a moral imperative but a business one, as diverse teams have been shown to be more innovative and effective. Understanding and navigating cultural differences, as well as being fluent in more than one language, can be significant assets.

Mental Health and Well-being

Finally, there's an increasing recognition of the importance of mental health and well-being in the workplace. Companies are implementing policies and practices to support work-life balance, reduce stress, and promote mental health. This trend reflects a broader understanding that employee well-being directly impacts productivity, engagement, and retention.

Understanding these trends is crucial for anyone looking to navigate the modern job market successfully. They influence not only the types of jobs available but also the skills required and the way we approach our careers. As we continue on this journey through the modern employment landscape, staying informed and adaptable will be key to transforming challenges into opportunities.

Chapter 2: The Alchemy of Skills Transformation

Identifying Your Core Competencies

In the labyrinth of career development, identifying your core competencies is akin to finding your compass; it's essential for navigating the modern job market with precision and purpose. These competencies are the bedrock of your professional identity, the unique blend of skills, abilities, and knowledge that set you apart in a competitive landscape. Understanding and articulating these strengths is not just about self-awareness; it's about strategically positioning yourself in a job market that values distinctiveness and specialization.

Defining Core Competencies

Core competencies are more than just skills; they are a combination of your capabilities, expertise, and personal traits that you excel in. They can include technical skills specific to your industry, but also encompass soft skills such as leadership, communication, and problem-solving. These competencies are the essence of what makes you effective in your role, the attributes that contribute to your unique value proposition as a professional.

Conducting a Self-Assessment

The journey to uncovering your core competencies begins with a thorough self-assessment. This introspective process involves reflecting on your past experiences, achievements, and the feedback you've received from peers, supervisors, and mentors. Ask yourself: In which projects did I excel? What tasks do I find both engaging and effortless? What skills have others consistently praised in me?

Utilizing tools like the SWOT analysis (Strengths, Weaknesses, Opportunities, Threats) can provide a structured framework for this self-assessment, helping you to identify not only your competencies but also areas for development and external opportunities to leverage them.

Seeking External Feedback

While self-reflection is critical, external feedback provides an invaluable perspective on your competencies. Reach out to colleagues, mentors, and former supervisors to gather insights about your strengths and areas where you've made significant impacts. This feedback can often reveal competencies that you may have overlooked or undervalued.

Analyzing Job Performance and Achievements

Your past job performances and key achievements are a goldmine for identifying your core competencies. Review your performance appraisals, project debriefs, and any accolades or recognitions you've received. Look for patterns in your successes and the skills that were pivotal in those scenarios. These patterns are indicative of your core competencies and can guide you in understanding where your professional strengths lie.

Understanding the Market Demand

Identifying your core competencies also involves understanding how they align with the current job market. Research the competencies that are in high demand within your industry and consider how your unique skill set matches these needs. This alignment not only helps in tailoring your career development efforts but also in positioning yourself as a valuable asset in the job market.

Continuous Development and Adaptation

It's important to recognize that core competencies are not static; they evolve as you progress in your career and as the market changes. Therefore, continuous learning and adaptation are key. Engage in professional development opportunities that not only strengthen your existing competencies but also help you develop new ones in response to emerging trends and technologies.

Articulating Your Core Competencies

Once identified, the ability to articulate your core competencies is crucial. Whether it's through your resume, in interviews, or networking opportunities, clearly communicating your strengths and how they translate to business value can set you apart. Use concrete examples and quantifiable achievements to demonstrate how your competencies have contributed to your success and the success of your organizations.

In conclusion, identifying your core competencies is a critical step in navigating the complexities of the modern job market. It requires introspection, feedback, and an understanding of market demands. By recognizing and articulating these competencies, you position yourself not just as a participant in the job market but as a standout candidate, poised to transform challenges into opportunities.

Adapting Your Skill Set for the Digital Age

In the swiftly evolving digital age, the ability to adapt your skill set is more than a necessity—it's a vital strategy for career longevity and success. The digital revolution has not only transformed the job market but also redefined the skills deemed essential for professionals across all industries. This era demands a blend of technical proficiency, digital literacy, and soft skills, all woven together with a mindset geared towards continuous learning and adaptability.

Embracing Digital Literacy

At the forefront of this transformation is digital literacy. It's no longer sufficient to be proficient in basic computer skills; today's professionals must be adept at leveraging a wide array of digital tools and platforms. From cloud-based collaboration software to sophisticated data analytics tools, understanding and utilizing these technologies is crucial. Digital literacy extends to the realm of cybersecurity awareness, understanding digital marketing principles, and being proficient in social media platforms, as these areas are integral to the modern business landscape.

Cultivating Technical Proficiency

For those in non-technical fields, the notion of technical proficiency might seem daunting. However, in the digital age, a basic understanding of technical concepts, such as coding, web development, and data analytics, can significantly enhance your professional profile. Platforms like Codecademy, Coursera, and Udemy offer accessible pathways to gaining these skills. Even a foundational knowledge of programming languages such as Python or JavaScript can open doors to new opportunities and collaborations.

Strengthening Soft Skills

While technical skills are undeniably important, the digital age also underscores the value of soft skills. Skills like critical thinking, problem-solving, effective communication, and adaptability are increasingly in demand as automation and AI take on more routine tasks. The ability to think strategically, work collaboratively across digital platforms, and lead with empathy in virtual environments are qualities that distinguish outstanding professionals in the digital landscape.

Data Literacy: The New Language of Business

Data has become the lifeblood of the modern economy, making data literacy an indispensable skill. Understanding how to interpret data, draw insights, and make data-driven decisions is becoming a standard requirement across job roles. Familiarizing yourself with basic data analysis tools and concepts can significantly enhance your decision-making process and increase your value to employers.

The Power of Continuous Learning

The digital age is characterized by rapid change, with new technologies and methodologies emerging at an unprecedented pace. This environment necessitates a commitment to lifelong learning. Embracing a mindset of growth and curiosity, and taking advantage of online learning platforms, workshops, and webinars can help you stay ahead of the curve. It's also beneficial to engage with professional communities and networks in your field to exchange knowledge and stay informed about the latest trends and best practices.

Adapting to Remote Work Environments

With the rise of remote work, mastering the art of virtual collaboration and communication has become essential. This includes not just familiarizing yourself with tools like Zoom, Slack, and Trello but also understanding the nuances of digital etiquette, remote team dynamics, and virtual leadership.

Personal Branding in the Digital World

In a landscape where your digital footprint can significantly impact your career opportunities, personal branding has taken on a new level of importance. Building a strong online presence, whether through a professional blog, LinkedIn profile, or industry-specific platforms, can showcase your skills and expertise to potential employers and collaborators worldwide.

Conclusion

Adapting your skill set for the digital age is a multifaceted endeavor, encompassing technical skills, soft skills, and a proactive approach to learning and personal development. By embracing digital literacy, committing to continuous education, and cultivating a versatile skill set, you can navigate the challenges and opportunities of the digital job market with confidence and agility. This adaptability not only positions you for success in your current role but also opens up a spectrum of future career possibilities in the dynamic landscape of the digital age.

Chapter 3: The Art of Job Searching in the Digital Era

Leveraging Online Platforms for Job Hunting

In the digital age, the landscape of job hunting has undergone a seismic shift, moving from traditional methods to a predominantly online ecosystem. Leveraging online platforms has become an indispensable strategy for those seeking to navigate the complexities of the modern job market. These platforms offer a plethora of tools and resources, making it easier than ever to connect with potential employers, discover opportunities, and showcase your professional brand.

Understanding the Digital Job Market Landscape

The digital job market is vast and varied, encompassing job boards, professional networking sites, company career pages, and social media platforms. Each of these serves a distinct purpose and offers unique advantages. Job boards like Indeed, Monster, and Glassdoor provide a wide array of listings and the ability to apply directly through the platform. Professional networking sites, with LinkedIn being the most prominent, offer the added benefit of networking opportunities, industry insights, and the ability to directly engage with hiring managers and recruiters.

Optimizing Your LinkedIn Profile

LinkedIn has emerged as a cornerstone of the digital job search. An optimized LinkedIn profile can significantly enhance your visibility and attractiveness to potential employers. This includes a professional photo, a compelling headline that captures your expertise and aspirations, and a detailed summary that narrates your professional story. Highlighting your experiences, skills, and achievements, along with recommendations and endorsements, can further solidify your credibility. Engaging with content, sharing industry insights, and actively participating in relevant groups can also increase your visibility and establish you as a thought leader in your field.

Utilizing Job Boards Effectively

Job boards remain a vital tool, but their effectiveness hinges on how they are used. Beyond simply applying for advertised positions, it's crucial to use these platforms to research companies, understand industry trends, and tailor your applications to specific job listings. Many job boards also offer tools for resume optimization, salary comparisons, and company reviews, providing a holistic view of potential employers.

Harnessing the Power of Niche Websites and Forums

Depending on your industry, niche websites and forums can be invaluable. Sites like AngelList for startups, Stack Overflow for developers, or Behance for creatives cater to specific professional communities, offering targeted job listings and networking opportunities. Engaging in these communities can not only lead to job opportunities but also provide insights into industry trends, challenges, and innovations.

Engaging with Company Career Pages

Many companies prefer to list their openings on their own career pages. Regularly visiting the career pages of companies you're interested in can provide insights into their culture, values, and the types of candidates they seek. It also shows initiative and a genuine interest in the company, traits that are highly valued by employers.

The Role of Social Media

Social media platforms like Twitter, Facebook, and Instagram are increasingly being used for job hunting. Following companies and industry leaders, engaging with their content, and sharing your professional achievements can catch the attention of potential employers. Additionally, many companies use these platforms to announce job openings, making them a valuable source of information.

Creating a Professional Online Presence

In the digital job market, your online presence is your resume. Creating a professional online presence that showcases your skills, achievements, and professional persona is crucial. This includes a professional blog, portfolio, or a personal website, depending on your industry. Ensuring consistency across platforms, from your LinkedIn profile to your personal website, reinforces your professional brand.

Staying Informed and Adaptable

The digital job market is ever-evolving, with new platforms and tools emerging regularly. Staying informed about the latest developments and being adaptable in your job search strategy is essential. Subscribing to industry newsletters, participating in webinars, and continuing to engage with professional communities can keep you abreast of new opportunities and trends.

In conclusion, leveraging online platforms for job hunting is not just about applying for jobs; it's about strategically positioning yourself in the digital job market, networking, and continuously enhancing your professional brand. By effectively utilizing these platforms, you can transform the daunting task of job hunting into a dynamic and fruitful endeavor, opening doors to myriad opportunities in the digital age.

Optimizing Your Digital Footprint

In today's interconnected world, your digital footprint is your virtual calling card; it's the sum total of your online activities and the digital trails you leave behind. Optimizing this footprint is paramount, not just for maintaining your online reputation, but for positioning yourself as an ideal candidate in the digital job market. This process is not about scrubbing your digital past clean; it's about strategically curating your online presence to align with your professional goals and personal brand.

Audit Your Online Presence

The first step in optimizing your digital footprint is to conduct a thorough audit of your online presence. This involves searching your name in various search engines and reviewing the information and images that appear. Pay close attention to social media profiles, blog posts, forum contributions, and any other content that's publicly associated with your name. The goal here is to ensure that the information available about you online is consistent, professional, and reflective of the image you wish to project to potential employers.

Professionalize Social Media Profiles

Social media platforms are often the first places potential employers will visit to learn more about you. It's crucial that your profiles on platforms like LinkedIn, Twitter, and Facebook present a professional image. On LinkedIn, ensure that your profile is complete with a professional photo, a compelling summary, and detailed descriptions of your work experience and achievements. Use this platform to showcase your expertise, share industry-relevant content, and engage with your network. For other social media platforms, consider adjusting your privacy settings to control what's visible to the public and ensure that any publicly visible content is appropriate and professional.

Create and Share Professional Content

One of the most effective ways to enhance your digital footprint is by creating and sharing professional content. This could include writing blog posts related to your field, sharing insightful articles on LinkedIn, or even creating informative videos or podcasts. Sharing your knowledge not only positions you as an expert in your field but also increases your visibility online. Engage with your audience by responding to comments and participating in discussions to further amplify your presence.

Engage in Professional Communities

Online professional communities and forums offer invaluable opportunities to network, share knowledge, and establish your presence within your industry. Platforms like Stack Overflow for developers, Behance for creatives, and numerous LinkedIn groups cater to professionals across various fields. Active participation in these communities can help you build connections, stay updated on industry trends, and contribute to discussions, further optimizing your digital footprint.

Manage Your Personal Brand

Your digital footprint is an extension of your personal brand. Consistency across platforms in terms of the content you share, the language you use, and the professional image you present is key. This consistency helps in building a coherent narrative about who you are as a professional and what you stand for. Regularly updating your profiles, sharing your achievements, and engaging with your network helps maintain a dynamic and attractive online persona.

Monitor Your Digital Footprint

Optimizing your digital footprint is an ongoing process. Regular monitoring and updating of your online presence are necessary to ensure it remains accurate, professional, and reflective of your current professional aspirations. Tools like Google Alerts can notify you when your name is mentioned online, allowing you to keep tabs on your digital footprint and address any issues promptly.

Digital Etiquette and Privacy

Understanding digital etiquette and managing your privacy settings across platforms is crucial. Be mindful of the comments you make, the content you share, and the interactions you have online. A respectful, professional demeanor goes a long way in maintaining a positive digital footprint. Additionally, familiarize yourself with the privacy settings on each platform to control the visibility of your personal information and posts.

In conclusion, optimizing your digital footprint in the digital age is not just about damage control; it's a strategic approach to crafting your online identity to support your career goals. By carefully curating your online presence, you can ensure that your digital footprint serves as a powerful asset in your job search and professional development, opening doors to opportunities and establishing your reputation in the digital job market.

Chapter 4: Networking and Personal Branding

Building a Professional Network Online and Offline

In the ever-evolving landscape of the modern job market, building a professional network has transcended traditional boundaries, merging online and offline realms into a comprehensive strategy for career growth. This fusion not only amplifies your visibility but also opens doors to opportunities that might otherwise remain hidden. A robust professional network serves as a lifeline in the tumultuous waters of career development, offering guidance, mentorship, and access to unadvertised job opportunities.

The Art of Networking Online

The digital era has revolutionized networking, making platforms like LinkedIn, Twitter, and industry-specific forums invaluable tools for connecting with professionals worldwide. To leverage these platforms effectively, it's crucial to approach online networking with intentionality and authenticity.

- **LinkedIn**: Start by optimizing your LinkedIn profile, ensuring it reflects your professional achievements and aspirations. Engage with your industry by sharing insightful articles, commenting on posts, and participating in discussions. Joining relevant LinkedIn groups and contributing to conversations can also enhance your visibility and establish your expertise.

- **Twitter and Other Social Media**: Twitter, while less formal than LinkedIn, offers a platform to follow industry leaders, engage with their content, and participate in industry-specific chats. Similarly, platforms like Instagram and Facebook, when used judically, can showcase your professional interests and personal brand.

- **Blogging and Content Creation**: Establishing a blog or a YouTube channel related to your field can significantly bolster your online presence. Sharing your knowledge and insights not only positions you as a thought leader but also attracts a network interested in your expertise.

Mastering Offline Networking

Despite the digital shift, the value of face-to-face interactions remains unparalleled. Offline networking involves a more personal touch, fostering deeper connections that can be instrumental in your career journey.

- **Industry Conferences and Events**: Attending conferences, workshops, and seminars related to your field is a golden opportunity to meet industry peers, leaders, and potential mentors. Be proactive in initiating conversations, and don't forget to follow up with new connections post-event through LinkedIn or email.

- **Professional Associations**: Joining professional associations can provide a structured environment for networking, offering regular meetings, industry insights, and access to exclusive job listings.

- **Alumni Networks**: Leveraging your alma mater's alumni network can open doors to connections with a shared background. Alumni events, reunions, and online forums are excellent venues for rekindling old ties and forging new ones.

Strategies for Effective Networking

- **Elevator Pitch**: Having a concise and compelling elevator pitch ready can help you introduce yourself effectively, highlighting your expertise and what you're seeking in your career.

- **Mutual Benefit**: Approach networking with a mindset of mutual benefit. Offer your help and support to your connections before asking for favors, establishing a foundation of reciprocity.

- **Consistency and Follow-Up**: Consistent engagement and timely follow-ups are key to maintaining and nurturing professional relationships. A simple check-in email or sharing an article of interest can keep the connection alive.

- **Mentorship**: Seek out mentors within your network who can provide guidance, feedback, and insights based on their experiences. A good mentor can be an invaluable asset in navigating career challenges and opportunities.

Networking Etiquette

Whether online or offline, maintaining professionalism and courtesy in all interactions is paramount. Respect people's time, express gratitude for their assistance, and always be ready to reciprocate help. Remember, networking is about building genuine relationships, not just collecting contacts.

In summary, building a professional network in today's digital age requires a strategic blend of online engagement and offline interactions. By leveraging the tools and platforms available, engaging with authenticity, and maintaining a reciprocal approach, you can create a network that supports your career aspirations, offers mentorship, and opens doors to opportunities that align with your professional journey.

Crafting an Authentic Personal Brand

In the tapestry of the modern professional world, an authentic personal brand stands as a beacon, guiding the narrative of your career and how you are perceived in the vast digital landscape. It's the amalgamation of your experiences, skills, values, and the unique flair you bring to your professional endeavors. Crafting this brand with intentionality and authenticity is not merely about self-promotion; it's about articulating your story, your aspirations, and the distinct value you offer, thereby resonating with potential employers, clients, and peers.

The Foundation of Your Personal Brand

At the heart of a compelling personal brand is authenticity. It begins with a deep, introspective dive into what defines you: your core values, passions, strengths, and the driving forces behind your career choices. This introspection is crucial, as it lays the groundwork for a brand that truly reflects who you are and what you stand for, ensuring that your professional persona is not just a façade, but a true representation of your individuality.

Articulating Your Unique Value Proposition

Your unique value proposition (UVP) is the cornerstone of your personal brand. It succinctly encapsulates what you excel at, the unique blend of skills and experiences you bring to the table, and how you differentiate yourself from others in your field. Crafting your UVP involves highlighting your achievements, skills, and the impact you've made in your roles, weaving these elements into a narrative that compellingly conveys your professional identity.

Consistency Across All Touchpoints

Consistency is key in personal branding. It's essential that every touchpoint — from your LinkedIn profile to your personal website, from your resume to your social media presence — conveys a cohesive message about who you are and what you offer. This consistency extends to the visual elements of your brand, such as professional headshots and a unified color scheme or design, ensuring that your brand is instantly recognizable across various platforms.

Engaging with Your Audience

An authentic personal brand is not a monologue; it's a dialogue with your audience. Engage with your professional community through thoughtful content, insightful comments, and meaningful interactions. Share your knowledge, celebrate the achievements of others, and contribute to discussions, all of which bolster your brand by demonstrating your expertise and your commitment to your professional community.

Showcasing Your Expertise

One of the most powerful ways to reinforce your personal brand is by showcasing your expertise. This can be through writing articles, giving presentations, participating in panel discussions, or any medium that allows you to share your knowledge and insights. These contributions not only highlight your expertise but also demonstrate your passion for your field and your willingness to contribute to the broader professional community.

Networking with Authenticity

Building and nurturing a professional network is an integral part of personal branding. Approach networking with a mindset of authenticity and genuine interest in others. Seek connections not just for the sake of expanding your network, but for the opportunity to learn from others, share insights, and collaborate on mutually beneficial endeavors.

Adapting and Evolving

Your personal brand, much like your career, is not static; it evolves as you grow professionally and personally. Regularly reflect on your brand, assessing whether it still accurately represents you and aligns with your current career aspirations. Be open to adapting and evolving your brand as you acquire new skills, shift your career focus, or redefine your professional goals.

Conclusion

Crafting an authentic personal brand is a strategic endeavor that demands introspection, consistency, and engagement. It's about more than just your online presence; it's about how you present yourself in every professional interaction, both online and offline. By developing a personal brand that truly reflects your unique value and engaging with your professional community with authenticity, you create a powerful tool that can open doors, attract opportunities, and pave the way for a fulfilling and dynamic career path.

Chapter 5: Innovative Job Applications

Creating Standout Resumes and Cover Letters

In the competitive arena of job hunting, crafting standout resumes and cover letters is akin to an art form, a strategic blend of personal branding, storytelling, and precision. These documents are not just formalities; they are your personal emissaries, making the first impression on potential employers and articulating your unique value proposition. Given their pivotal role, it's imperative to approach them with a blend of creativity, authenticity, and strategic thoughtfulness.

The Art of Crafting a Standout Resume

Your resume is more than a list of jobs and educational achievements; it's a curated showcase of your journey, skills, and accomplishments. To elevate it from a mere document to a compelling narrative:

- **Tailor Your Resume**: One size does not fit all. Customize your resume for each job application, emphasizing the skills and experiences most relevant to the position.

- **Clear and Concise Formatting**: Adopt a clean, professional layout that allows for easy scanning. Use bullet points to break down achievements and responsibilities, and ensure your contact information is prominently displayed.

- **Highlight Achievements, Not Just Duties**: Quantify your achievements with specific metrics where possible. Instead of stating you "managed a team," specify "led a team of 10 to achieve a 20% increase in efficiency."

- **Incorporate Keywords**: Many companies use Applicant Tracking Systems (ATS) to screen resumes. Include keywords from the job description to ensure your resume passes through these digital gatekeepers.

- **Professional Summary**: Start with a compelling professional summary that encapsulates your professional identity, core competencies, and what you bring to the table.

- **Use Action Verbs**: Begin bullet points with dynamic action verbs like "spearheaded," "innovated," or "transformed" to convey a proactive, results-oriented approach.

The Power of a Persuasive Cover Letter

While your resume sketches the outline of your professional landscape, your cover letter fills in the colors, providing context, depth, and personality. It's your chance to speak directly to the hiring manager, making a compelling case for why you're the ideal candidate.

- **Personalize Your Greeting**: Whenever possible, address the cover letter to a specific person. This demonstrates attention to detail and a personalized approach.

- **Tell Your Story**: Use the cover letter to narrate your professional journey, highlighting how your experiences align with the company's needs and culture. This is your opportunity to connect the dots between your past achievements and your future potential.

- **Show Enthusiasm for the Role**: Convey genuine enthusiasm for the position and the company. Illustrate your knowledge about the company's challenges and how you can contribute to solving them.

- **Call to Action**: End with a proactive call to action, expressing your eagerness to discuss how you can contribute to the team and the value you'll bring to the role.

Leveraging Digital Enhancements

In the digital age, consider supplementing your resume and cover letter with digital enhancements. This could include links to your LinkedIn profile, professional portfolio, or personal website. For creative roles, infographics or video resumes can offer a dynamic and interactive overview of your skills and experiences.

Feedback and Iteration

Before finalizing your documents, seek feedback from mentors, peers, or professionals in your field. A fresh set of eyes can offer invaluable insights and help polish your resume and cover letter to perfection. Be open to revising and refining your documents based on the feedback received.

Conclusion

Creating standout resumes and cover letters is a critical step in your job search journey. These documents should not only showcase your qualifications and achievements but also reflect your personality, professionalism, and the unique value you bring to potential employers. By crafting these documents with care, creativity, and strategic alignment with your career goals, you set the stage for successful engagements in the job market, paving the way for opportunities that align with your professional aspirations and values.

The Power of Storytelling in Job Applications

In the realm of job applications, the power of storytelling is transformative, turning standard submissions into compelling narratives that capture the essence of your professional journey. It's not merely about listing your qualifications and experiences; it's about weaving those elements into a narrative that resonates with potential employers, highlighting not just what you've done, but who you are and how you approach challenges and opportunities.

Crafting Your Professional Story

Every career is a story, filled with challenges, achievements, learning moments, and milestones. Start by reflecting on your career path: the pivotal moments, the decisions that shaped your journey, the challenges you overcame, and the successes you achieved. These elements form the chapters of your professional story, providing a rich tapestry that goes beyond a mere resume.

Integrating Stories into Your Resume

While a resume might seem like an unlikely place for storytelling, there are strategic ways to infuse narrative elements. Begin with a strong summary statement that encapsulates your professional identity and value proposition, setting the stage for your story. For each role you've held, go beyond listing duties; describe the context, the challenges you faced, the actions you took, and, most importantly, the outcomes and impact of those actions. Use quantifiable achievements to underscore the narrative, making your contributions tangible and relatable.

Elevating Your Cover Letter Through Narrative

Your cover letter offers a prime opportunity to tell your story directly to potential employers. Use this space to connect the dots of your resume, providing context and depth to your experiences. Share a compelling story from your career that highlights your problem-solving skills, resilience, or ability to lead and inspire others. This narrative should illuminate your unique strengths and how they align with the company's values and goals.

Showcasing Soft Skills Through Stories

Soft skills, such as leadership, teamwork, adaptability, and creativity, are often intangible and hard to quantify. Storytelling allows you to illustrate these skills in action. For instance, recount a time when your creative thinking solved a complex problem or when your leadership steered a project to success against all odds. These stories provide a dynamic portrayal of your soft skills, making them vivid and memorable.

Personalizing Stories for the Role

Tailoring your stories to the role and company is crucial. Research the company's culture, values, and challenges, and choose stories that reflect how you can contribute and thrive in that environment. This personalization shows that you're not just looking for any job, but that you're invested in this specific opportunity and have thought deeply about your fit within the organization.

Using Stories in Interviews

The narrative approach extends to interviews, where you can bring your stories to life through conversation. Prepare a repertoire of stories that you can adapt to different questions, whether it's about leadership, teamwork, overcoming challenges, or learning from failure. This not only makes your responses more engaging but also helps interviewers envision you in the role, contributing to the team and company.

Maintaining Authenticity

Authenticity is the cornerstone of effective storytelling. Your stories should be true reflections of your experiences, told with sincerity and genuine emotion. Authentic stories resonate more deeply, fostering a connection with the listener and leaving a lasting impression.

Conclusion

The power of storytelling in job applications lies in its ability to transform how you're perceived by potential employers. It's about painting a picture of yourself not just as a candidate with a certain set of skills and experiences, but as a dynamic individual with a unique story, ready to bring your full self to the role. By mastering the art of storytelling, you can elevate your job applications, making them not just informative, but truly compelling and memorable.

Chapter 6: Acing the Modern Job Interview

Preparing for Virtual and In-person Interviews

In the evolving landscape of the job market, mastering both virtual and in-person interviews has become essential. These interviews, while sharing a common goal, require nuanced preparations to navigate their unique dynamics effectively. The ability to adapt and excel in both settings can significantly enhance your chances of making a lasting impression and securing your desired role.

Mastering the Art of Virtual Interviews

Virtual interviews, a staple in the digital age's recruitment process, demand a unique set of considerations:

- **Technical Setup**: Ensure your computer, camera, and microphone are in good working condition. Conduct a test run on the platform to be used for the interview to familiarize yourself with its features and avoid technical glitches.

- **Environment**: Choose a quiet, well-lit space with a neutral background. Consider the lighting carefully; natural light is preferable, but if that's not possible, ensure the light source is in front of you, illuminating your face clearly.

- **Dress Code**: Dress professionally, as you would for an in-person interview, to convey seriousness and respect for the opportunity. This also helps put you in the right mindset for the interview.

- **Body Language and Eye Contact**: Maintain good posture and stay engaged. Since making eye contact can be challenging in virtual settings, practice looking at the camera to simulate eye contact, creating a sense of connection and attentiveness.

- **Minimize Distractions**: Inform others in your household of your interview to avoid interruptions. Turn off notifications on your computer and phone to maintain focus.

Navigating In-person Interviews

In-person interviews offer a direct, personal connection, making the preparation for them distinct:

- **First Impressions**: Arrive early, dressed appropriately for the company's culture. A firm handshake, a warm smile, and maintaining eye contact upon greeting your interviewers set a positive tone.

- **Non-verbal Cues**: Be mindful of your body language throughout the interview. Sit up straight, nod to show understanding, and use hand gestures naturally to express yourself.

- **Materials**: Bring copies of your resume, a list of references, and a notebook for jotting down notes. Having these at hand demonstrates your preparedness and professionalism.

Common Grounds for Both Interview Types

While virtual and in-person interviews have their unique aspects, several preparation strategies are universally applicable:

- **Research**: Deep dive into the company's history, culture, values, and recent achievements. Understanding the company allows you to tailor your responses and questions to align with their ethos.

- **Practice**: Rehearse your answers to common interview questions, but avoid memorizing them to prevent sounding robotic. Use the STAR method (Situation, Task, Action, Result) to structure your answers effectively.

- **Questions for Interviewers**: Prepare insightful questions to ask your interviewers. This demonstrates your interest in the role and the company and helps you assess if the opportunity aligns with your career goals.

- **Mindset and Attitude**: Approach the interview with confidence and a positive attitude. Remember, the interview is also an opportunity for you to evaluate if the company and the role are a good fit for you.

- **Follow-up**: Send a personalized thank-you email within 24 hours of the interview, reiterating your interest in the position and expressing gratitude for the opportunity to interview.

Conclusion

Whether virtual or in-person, interviews are a critical component of the job application process. They offer a platform to showcase not just your qualifications and experiences but also your personality, professionalism, and fit for the role and the company. By meticulously preparing for both types of interviews, you equip yourself with the confidence and skills needed to excel and leave a lasting impression on your potential employers, bringing you one step closer to securing your desired position in the dynamic employment arena.

Behavioral Interviewing Techniques

In the intricate dance of the modern job interview, mastering behavioral interviewing techniques is akin to learning the steps to a complex, yet rewarding, dance. It's a method that goes beyond the surface, delving into past behaviors and experiences as predictors of future performance. As we navigate this dance floor, it's essential to understand the rhythm and nuances of behavioral interviewing, preparing ourselves to respond with authenticity, precision, and depth.

Understanding Behavioral Interviews

Behavioral interviews are grounded in the philosophy that past behavior is the most reliable indicator of future performance in similar situations. This approach seeks to explore how you've handled specific work-related scenarios, providing a lens into your problem-solving abilities, adaptability, leadership qualities, and other competencies crucial to the role at hand.

The STAR Method

The STAR method stands as a beacon in the realm of behavioral interviewing, offering a structured approach to formulating responses. It stands for Situation, Task, Action, and Result:

- **Situation**: Begin by setting the stage. Describe a specific situation or challenge you faced in a previous role. Provide enough detail to give the interviewer a clear picture but keep it concise.

- **Task**: Outline the task or objective that was at hand. What was required of you? What goals were you working towards?

- **Action**: This is the heart of your story. Detail the specific actions you took to address the situation or task. Focus on your contributions, even if the scenario was a team effort. Use "I" statements to highlight your role.

- **Result**: Conclude with the outcome of your actions. Quantify the results where possible, using data or specific achievements to underscore the impact of your actions. Reflect on what you learned from the experience.

Preparing Your Behavioral Arsenal

To excel in behavioral interviews, preparation is key. Reflect on your career, identifying a range of scenarios that showcase your skills and achievements. Consider challenges you've overcome, leadership experiences, times when you've gone above and beyond, and instances of innovation and problem-solving. Develop a diverse portfolio of stories, ensuring you have a well-rounded selection to draw from.

Tailoring Your Responses

While it's beneficial to have a repertoire of stories, tailor your selection to the role and company. Prior to the interview, analyze the job description and company values, identifying key competencies and traits they value. Choose stories that best reflect these attributes, demonstrating your alignment with the company's culture and the role's requirements.

Practicing Your Delivery

The impact of your stories is not just in their content but in their delivery. Practice recounting your stories, focusing on clarity, conciseness, and engagement. Ensure your narratives are compelling and articulate, avoiding unnecessary jargon or tangents. Seek feedback from mentors or peers to refine your storytelling skills.

Reflecting on Learnings and Growth

In your narratives, don't shy away from discussing challenges or even failures, provided they lead to learning and growth. Reflecting on what you've learned from past experiences demonstrates self-awareness, resilience, and a growth mindset—qualities highly valued in any professional setting.

Engaging with Authenticity

While preparation is crucial, it's equally important to engage with authenticity. Let your personality and genuine passion shine through your stories. Authentic responses not only make your narratives more relatable but also help build a connection with the interviewer.

Conclusion

Behavioral interviewing techniques offer a powerful tool in the job seeker's arsenal, allowing you to showcase your experiences, skills, and personal qualities in a structured and impactful manner. By understanding the nuances of behavioral interviews, preparing your stories with the STAR method, and engaging with authenticity and precision, you equip yourself to navigate these interviews with confidence. This preparation not only enhances your chances of success but also provides a deeper insight into your own professional journey, reinforcing your readiness to tackle future challenges and opportunities in your career path.

Chapter 7: Navigating Job Offers and Negotiations

Evaluating Job Offers Beyond Salary

In the intricate dance of career advancement, receiving a job offer is a moment of triumph, yet it's just the beginning of a crucial decision-making process. It's imperative to look beyond the surface allure of a salary figure and delve into the broader spectrum of factors that contribute to genuine job satisfaction and career growth. Evaluating a job offer in its entirety requires a holistic approach, considering not just the immediate benefits but the long-term impact on your professional journey and personal fulfillment.

Understanding the Full Compensation Package

The total compensation package extends far beyond the base salary. It encompasses bonuses, stock options, profit-sharing plans, and other financial incentives. Scrutinize these elements closely, understanding their potential value and how they align with your financial goals and risk tolerance. Additionally, benefits such as health insurance, retirement plans, and paid time off contribute significantly to your overall compensation and should be carefully evaluated.

Work-Life Balance and Flexibility

In today's fast-paced world, the importance of work-life balance cannot be overstated. Consider the job's demands, including expected work hours, flexibility, remote work options, and the company's culture around work-life integration. Organizations that value and promote a healthy balance tend to have higher employee satisfaction and retention rates.

Career Development and Growth Opportunities

A pivotal aspect of any job offer is the opportunity it presents for learning and growth. Investigate the company's commitment to professional development, availability of mentorship programs, and pathways for advancement within the organization. A role that offers room for growth and aligns with your career aspirations can be more valuable in the long run than a higher-paying position with limited advancement opportunities.

Company Culture and Values

The congruence between your personal values and the company's culture is fundamental to your job satisfaction. Research the company's mission, values, and work environment. Consider how decision-making is approached, how achievements are recognized, and how challenges are addressed. Engage with current or former employees if possible, to gain insights into the company's culture and management style.

The Team and Leadership

The dynamics of the team you'll be joining and the leadership style of your potential supervisors can significantly influence your work experience. During the interview process, try to meet with key team members and leaders to gauge the team's cohesion, communication style, and overall atmosphere. A supportive and collaborative team under effective leadership can greatly enhance job satisfaction.

Location and Commute

The physical location of the job and the commute it entails are practical considerations that can impact your daily life. Assess the commute time, convenience, and associated costs, considering how they align with your lifestyle and preferences. For remote positions, evaluate the support system in place for remote employees and how the company fosters a sense of inclusion and connectivity among its dispersed workforce.

Impact and Contribution

Consider the potential impact of your role within the company and beyond. Evaluate how the position allows you to contribute to meaningful projects, innovate, and make a difference. Roles that align with your passions and enable you to make a significant impact can offer a deeper sense of fulfillment and motivation.

Conclusion

Evaluating a job offer is a multifaceted process that extends well beyond salary considerations. It's about envisioning your future within the company, assessing how the role aligns with your personal and professional goals, and determining the potential for growth and fulfillment. By taking a comprehensive approach to evaluate job offers, you position yourself to make informed decisions that not only advance your career but also enrich your life, steering your professional journey towards rewarding horizons.

Negotiation Strategies for the Modern Workplace

Navigating the negotiation process in the modern workplace is a critical skill that can significantly impact your career trajectory and overall job satisfaction. It's about striking a balance between your value and aspirations and the opportunities and constraints within the organization. Effective negotiation requires preparation, clear communication, and a mindset geared towards finding mutually beneficial solutions.

Preparation: Laying the Groundwork

The foundation of any successful negotiation is thorough preparation. Start by researching industry standards for the role, taking into account factors like your experience, geographic location, and the company's size. Tools like Glassdoor, PayScale, and LinkedIn Salary can provide valuable insights.

Understanding the company's position is equally important. Gauge their priorities, challenges, and limitations. This knowledge not only informs your approach but also helps in tailoring your requests to align with the company's goals and constraints.

Articulating Your Value

Your ability to articulate your value is pivotal. Reflect on your achievements, skills, and the unique contributions you can bring to the role. Be ready to share specific examples that demonstrate your impact in previous positions, using quantifiable results whenever possible. This isn't just about past successes; it's about conveying how your unique value proposition is relevant to the needs and goals of the company.

Strategic Conversation Starters

Initiating the negotiation conversation with tact and professionalism sets a positive tone for the discussion. Express your enthusiasm for the role and the company before transitioning into negotiation. A statement like, "I'm genuinely excited about the opportunity to contribute to the team and am keen to find a package that reflects the value I bring to the role" can be an effective opener.

Focusing on the Total Package

Beyond salary, consider the total compensation package, including benefits, work-life balance, professional development opportunities, and other perks. Sometimes, there may be more flexibility in areas outside of the base salary. Identify which components are most important to you and be prepared to discuss these preferences.

Employing Effective Negotiation Techniques

- **Use of Silence**: After making a request, allow for silence. This gives the other party time to consider your proposal and can often lead to more favorable outcomes.

- **The "If...Then" Technique**: This involves framing your requests in a way that shows you're looking for solutions, not just making demands. For example, "If we can't meet that salary level, then could we explore a signing bonus or an earlier performance review?"

- **Expressing Flexibility**: Show that you're open to creative solutions. Phrases like "I'm open to suggestions" and "Let's find a solution that works for both of us" demonstrate flexibility and a collaborative spirit.

Handling Pushback with Grace

Not all negotiations will go smoothly. If you encounter resistance, respond with professionalism and poise. Seek to understand the other party's concerns and constraints, and use this as a basis for further discussion. Remember, negotiation is a process, not a one-time event.

Knowing When to Compromise

While it's important to advocate for your worth and needs, it's also crucial to know when to compromise. Evaluate the overall opportunity, considering career growth, the work environment, and how the role aligns with your long-term goals. Sometimes, the strategic career move might involve accepting an offer that isn't perfect but offers significant long-term benefits.

Conclusion

Negotiation in the modern workplace is an intricate dance that requires preparation, clear communication, and a collaborative mindset. By thoroughly preparing, articulating your value, and employing strategic negotiation techniques, you can navigate these conversations with confidence and tact. Remember, the goal is not just to reach an agreement but to lay the foundation for a positive and productive working relationship.

Chapter 8: Thriving in the Gig Economy

Opportunities and Challenges of Freelancing

Embarking on a freelance career represents a significant shift from traditional employment, offering a unique blend of opportunities and challenges that can redefine one's professional journey. As someone who has navigated the complexities of various job markets, I've come to appreciate the nuanced landscape of freelancing, which is characterized by its flexibility, potential for diversity in projects, and the autonomy it offers. However, it also demands a high level of self-discipline, proactive business development skills, and the ability to navigate the uncertainty inherent in this career path.

The Freedom of Flexibility

One of the most enticing aspects of freelancing is the unparalleled flexibility it provides. You have the autonomy to choose your projects, set your schedule, and work from virtually anywhere. This level of control can lead to a more balanced lifestyle, allowing you to tailor your work environment and schedule to fit personal commitments and preferences. However, this freedom comes with the responsibility of self-management, requiring you to be adept at time management and maintaining productivity without the external structure provided by a traditional office setting.

Diverse Projects and Continuous Learning

Freelancing opens the door to a wide array of projects across different industries, offering a platform for continuous learning and professional growth. This diversity can be incredibly enriching, allowing you to apply your skills in varied contexts and continually expand your expertise. Yet, the onus is on you to seek out these opportunities, pitch your services effectively, and maintain a pipeline of work that ensures financial stability.

Building and Leveraging Your Network

A robust professional network is the backbone of a successful freelance career. Networking opportunities, both online and offline, are crucial for finding new projects, building collaborations, and gaining referrals. Effective networking requires consistent effort and genuine engagement with your professional community, highlighting the importance of crafting an authentic personal brand and establishing a strong online presence.

Navigating Financial Uncertainty

One of the most significant challenges in freelancing is managing financial uncertainty. The feast-or-famine nature of freelance work necessitates meticulous financial planning, including setting aside savings for lean periods, managing irregular income streams, and planning for taxes and retirement independently. This aspect of freelancing demands a proactive approach to financial management, underscoring the need to diversify income sources and maintain a buffer for unforeseen circumstances.

Setting Boundaries and Ensuring Well-being

Without the clear boundaries provided by a traditional job, freelancers must be vigilant in setting limits to prevent burnout. This includes establishing clear work hours, creating a dedicated workspace, and ensuring time for rest and recreation. The blurring of work-life boundaries can be a slippery slope, making it imperative to consciously cultivate a healthy work-life balance.

Continuous Skill Development

In the fast-paced freelance market, staying relevant requires an ongoing commitment to skill development and adaptation. This encompasses not only honing your craft but also developing business skills such as marketing, negotiation, and client management. The onus is on the freelancer to identify emerging trends, invest in learning new skills, and continuously adapt to the evolving demands of the market.

Conclusion

The freelance landscape offers a realm of possibilities for those willing to navigate its challenges. It promises the freedom to carve out a career that aligns with one's values, lifestyle, and professional aspirations. Yet, it demands resilience, adaptability, and a proactive stance towards personal and professional development. Embracing freelancing is not just about choosing a non-traditional career path; it's about adopting a mindset geared towards growth, flexibility, and continuous evolution in the face of the ever-changing dynamics of the modern job market.

Building a Sustainable Career in the Gig Economy

Navigating the gig economy's waters requires a strategic approach, blending adaptability with a keen focus on long-term sustainability. As I've delved into various employment landscapes, the gig economy stands out for its dynamic nature, offering a plethora of opportunities while also presenting unique challenges. The key to thriving in this environment lies in understanding its intricacies and adopting practices that ensure not just immediate success but enduring career growth.

Embracing the Gig Economy's Flexibility

The gig economy's hallmark is its flexibility, allowing professionals to choose projects that align with their skills, interests, and lifestyle preferences. This flexibility, however, should be balanced with strategic planning. It's crucial to set clear professional goals and align gig work with these objectives, ensuring each project contributes to building a cohesive portfolio that showcases your expertise and advances your career.

Diversification: The Safety Net

Diversification is more than a buzzword in the gig economy; it's a necessity. Relying on a single income stream or client can be precarious. Cultivating a diverse client base and skill set not only mitigates risk but also opens up new opportunities for growth. This involves continuously scanning the market for emerging trends and upskilling accordingly, ensuring your services remain in demand.

Financial Planning for Stability

The fluctuating income inherent in gig work demands astute financial planning. Establishing a budget that accommodates variable earnings, setting aside savings for lean periods, and planning for taxes, health insurance, and retirement are foundational steps in creating financial stability. Tools and apps designed for freelancers can aid in tracking expenses, invoicing, and financial forecasting, helping maintain a steady financial course.

Building and Nurturing Your Network

In the gig economy, your network is your lifeline. It's not just a source of new projects; it's a support system, a sounding board, and at times, a collaborative partner. Investing time in building and nurturing professional relationships is essential. Attend industry events, engage in online communities, and don't underestimate the power of word-of-mouth referrals. A strong network can propel your freelance career to new heights.

Crafting a Compelling Personal Brand

Your personal brand is your calling card in the gig economy. It communicates your unique value proposition, attracting clients who are a good fit for your skills and working style. An authentic and well-crafted personal brand, reinforced by a professional online presence and consistent communication style, sets you apart in a crowded marketplace.

Prioritizing Work-Life Harmony

The blur between personal and professional life is a common challenge in gig work. Setting boundaries is essential for maintaining work-life harmony. This includes defining clear work hours, creating a dedicated workspace, and making time for rest and rejuvenation. Remember, sustainability is not just about professional endurance; it's also about personal well-being.

Leveraging Technology for Efficiency

Technology is a powerful ally in managing the complexities of gig work. From project management tools and communication platforms to time tracking and invoicing software, leveraging the right technology can streamline operations, enhance productivity, and allow you to focus more on your core competencies.

Advocacy and Continuous Learning

Staying informed about the legal and economic aspects of freelancing, including rights, contracts, and industry standards, is crucial. Additionally, a commitment to continuous learning, through online courses, workshops, and networking, ensures you remain competitive and can pivot as the market evolves.

Conclusion

Building a sustainable career in the gig economy is an exercise in balance, blending the freedom and diversity of gig work with strategic planning, financial acumen, and a focus on long-term growth. By embracing the unique dynamics of the gig economy while adopting practices that ensure stability and growth, you can craft a fulfilling and resilient career path that not only meets your immediate needs but also sets the foundation for future success.

Chapter 9: Continuous Learning and Career Development

Embracing Lifelong Learning

In the dynamic tapestry of today's employment landscape, the concept of lifelong learning has transcended being merely advantageous—it has become indispensable. The velocity at which industries evolve, spurred by relentless technological advancements and shifting global paradigms, mandates a perpetual state of learning and adaptation. As I navigate through the myriad pathways of career development, I've come to recognize that embracing lifelong learning is not just about acquiring new skills; it's about fostering a mindset attuned to continuous growth, resilience, and the agility to navigate the complexities of modern employment arenas.

Cultivating a Growth Mindset

At the heart of lifelong learning lies the cultivation of a growth mindset—a belief in the boundless potential to expand one's abilities and intelligence. This mindset encourages viewing challenges as opportunities for growth, fostering resilience in the face of setbacks, and viewing effort as a pathway to mastery. It's about shifting from a perspective of "I can't do this" to "I can't do this *yet*," embracing the journey of learning as an integral part of personal and professional development.

Staying Abreast of Industry Trends

The modern job market is characterized by its fluidity, with emerging technologies and evolving business models reshaping industries. Staying informed about these trends is crucial. This involves regular engagement with industry publications, attending webinars and conferences, and participating in professional networks. Such proactive engagement not only keeps you informed but also inspires innovation and creative thinking in your approach to challenges and opportunities.

Leveraging Digital Platforms for Learning

The digital age has democratized access to knowledge, with a plethora of resources available at our fingertips. Online learning platforms like Coursera, Udemy, and LinkedIn Learning offer courses across a vast spectrum of subjects, taught by industry experts. These platforms provide the flexibility to learn at one's own pace, making it feasible to integrate learning into even the busiest of schedules. Moreover, many institutions offer free or low-cost access to their coursework, making continuous education accessible to a broader audience.

Building a Personal Learning Network

A personal learning network (PLN) is a vibrant ecosystem of relationships with individuals and organizations that inspire, challenge, and contribute to one's learning journey. This network might include mentors, peers, online forums, and social media groups. Engaging with your PLN through discussions, collaboration on projects, or sharing insights not only enriches your learning experience but also enhances your professional visibility and connectivity.

Learning Through Teaching

One of the most profound ways to solidify new knowledge and skills is to teach others. Whether it's leading a workshop, writing a blog post, or mentoring a colleague, teaching forces you to distill your understanding into coherent, accessible concepts. This process not only reinforces your own learning but also contributes to the collective knowledge pool of your professional community.

Reflective Practice and Continuous Feedback

Reflective practice involves taking a step back to contemplate the experiences and lessons learned through professional endeavors. Coupled with seeking and acting on feedback, this practice can illuminate areas for improvement and guide your learning priorities. It's a cyclical process of action, reflection, learning, and growth.

Embracing Change and Uncertainty

The modern employment landscape is inherently uncertain, with change being the only constant. Lifelong learning equips individuals to navigate this uncertainty with confidence, viewing change not as a threat but as an opportunity for growth. It's about developing the agility to pivot when necessary, leveraging the skills and knowledge acquired through continuous learning to adapt to new roles, industries, or entrepreneurial ventures.

Conclusion

In essence, embracing lifelong learning is about adopting a proactive stance towards your own development, recognizing that the journey of learning is perpetual and intertwined with the fabric of a fulfilling career. It's a commitment to not just keeping pace with the evolving job market but thriving within it, armed with the resilience, adaptability, and curiosity that lifelong learning fosters. This ethos of continuous growth and development is at the core of navigating the challenges and seizing the opportunities presented by today's dynamic employment arena, paving the way for a career that is not only successful but also deeply rewarding.

Strategies for Career Growth and Adaptation

In the ever-evolving tapestry of the modern job market, the ability to grow and adapt is not just an asset; it's a necessity. The landscape we navigate today is markedly different from what it was even a decade ago, shaped by rapid technological advancements, shifting economic forces, and the increasingly global nature of business. As I reflect on my journey and the insights gained through extensive research and practical experience, it's clear that intentional strategies for career growth and adaptation are paramount for anyone looking to thrive in this dynamic environment.

Setting Clear Career Goals

The first step in any strategy for career growth is to define clear, actionable goals. These should be both aspirational and achievable, providing a north star for your career journey while allowing for flexibility as circumstances evolve. Setting SMART goals—Specific, Measurable, Achievable, Relevant, and Time-bound—can provide structure and direction, helping to navigate the complexities of career development with purpose and clarity.

Embracing a Proactive Learning Ethos

The cornerstone of career adaptation is a commitment to lifelong learning. In a world where new technologies and methodologies can quickly render yesterday's expertise obsolete, staying abreast of industry trends and continuously upgrading skills is essential. This might mean pursuing formal education, such as advanced degrees or certifications, or leveraging informal learning opportunities, like online courses, webinars, and industry conferences. Cultivating a proactive learning ethos ensures that you remain competitive and relevant, regardless of how your field evolves.

Building a Robust Professional Network

Networking remains one of the most effective strategies for career growth. A robust professional network can provide not just opportunities for new roles or projects but also insights into industry trends, access to mentors and thought leaders, and support from peers facing similar challenges. Prioritize building genuine relationships based on mutual respect and value exchange, and don't underestimate the power of online platforms like LinkedIn to connect with professionals across the globe.

Cultivating Adaptability and Resilience

Adaptability and resilience are key to navigating the uncertainties of the modern job market. This means being open to change, whether it's a shift in your role, a pivot to a new industry, or the need to retrain in response to emerging technologies. Developing a mindset that views challenges as opportunities for growth can transform potential setbacks into stepping stones, fostering a career path characterized by resilience and continuous evolution.

Leveraging Personal Branding

In today's digital age, personal branding has become an integral part of career strategy. Your personal brand communicates your unique value proposition, helping you stand out in a crowded job market. It's about more than just your online presence; it's the narrative thread that connects your skills, experiences, and professional ethos. Invest time in crafting a personal brand that authentically represents you and resonates with your target audience, whether that's potential employers, clients, or collaborators.

Strategic Career Pivots

There may come a time in your career when a pivot becomes necessary or desirable. This could be a transition to a new role within your field, a leap into a different industry, or even the launch of an entrepreneurial venture. Strategic career pivots require thorough research, careful planning, and often, the courage to step outside your comfort zone. Seek advice from mentors, leverage your network for insights and opportunities, and approach the pivot with a mindset geared towards learning and growth.

Feedback and Reflective Practice

Regular feedback is invaluable for career growth, providing insights into your strengths, areas for improvement, and the impact of your work. Cultivate relationships with mentors and peers who can provide honest, constructive feedback, and engage in regular self-reflection to assess your progress towards your goals. Reflective practice, combined with feedback, can illuminate the path forward, guiding your decisions and strategies for career development.

Conclusion

Strategies for career growth and adaptation in the modern job market are multifaceted, requiring clarity of purpose, a commitment to learning, the cultivation of a strong network, and the resilience to navigate change. By embracing these strategies, you can not only navigate the challenges of today's employment landscape but also seize the opportunities it presents, crafting a career that is not only successful but also fulfilling and aligned with your personal and professional aspirations.

Conclusion: The Future of Work and Employment

Predictions for the Evolving Job Market

As we stand on the brink of unprecedented changes in the job market, propelled by rapid technological advancements, globalization, and shifting societal norms, the future of work seems both exhilarating and daunting. Drawing from extensive research and my experiences navigating the complexities of employment trends, I foresee several pivotal shifts that will redefine the landscape of work in the coming years.

The Rise of AI and Automation

Artificial Intelligence (AI) and automation are poised to reshape the job market fundamentally. While concerns about job displacement are valid, it's crucial to recognize the potential for these technologies to create new roles and industries, much like the internet did. We'll see a surge in demand for roles that oversee, complement, and enhance AI capabilities, including jobs in AI ethics, machine learning oversight, and human-AI collaboration specialists. The key will be to adapt to this change by embracing skills that AI cannot replicate—creativity, emotional intelligence, and complex problem-solving.

The Gig Economy and Freelance Work

The gig economy will continue to expand, offering unprecedented flexibility and autonomy for workers. However, this shift also necessitates a reevaluation of traditional employment benefits and protections. I predict a move towards more robust support structures for gig workers, including portable benefits and regulations that ensure fair wages and working conditions. This evolution will require a delicate balance between preserving the flexibility that defines gig work and providing a safety net for those who pursue it.

Remote Work and Global Teams

The normalization of remote work is dismantling geographical barriers, enabling organizations to tap into global talent pools. This shift towards distributed teams will require enhanced digital communication skills, cultural competency, and a new approach to leadership that emphasizes trust and outcomes over traditional oversight. As remote work becomes more prevalent, we'll see innovations in virtual collaboration tools and methodologies, making distance increasingly irrelevant to effective teamwork.

Lifelong Learning and Skill Adaptation

The half-life of professional skills is rapidly shrinking, necessitating a culture of continuous learning and adaptation. Organizations will increasingly invest in upskilling and reskilling their workforce, while individuals will take a more proactive role in their learning journeys. The educational landscape will evolve to support this, with micro-credentials, online learning platforms, and industry-academia partnerships becoming integral to professional development.

Emphasis on Sustainability and Social Responsibility

As societal awareness of environmental and social issues grows, so too will the demand for jobs that address these challenges. Sustainability will become a core component of every industry, creating roles focused on green technologies, sustainable supply chain management, and corporate social responsibility. Professionals who can combine their domain expertise with a deep understanding of sustainability principles will be highly sought after.

Enhanced Focus on Mental Health and Well-Being

The increasing recognition of mental health's impact on productivity and job satisfaction will lead to more holistic approaches to work-life balance. Companies will prioritize creating environments that support well-being, including flexible work arrangements, mental health resources, and cultures that value rest and recovery as much as performance.

Conclusion

As we navigate the complexities of the evolving job market, adaptability, foresight, and a commitment to lifelong learning will be paramount. The changes ahead offer an opportunity to rethink not just how we work, but why we work, and what we value in our careers. By staying attuned to these shifts and embracing the principles of modern job alchemy, we can transform challenges into opportunities, crafting careers that are not only successful but also fulfilling and aligned with the broader changes shaping our world.

Cultivating Resilience and Adaptability

In the fluid and often unpredictable landscape of today's job market, resilience and adaptability are not just beneficial traits—they are essential to thriving amidst constant change. Drawing from my extensive exploration of employment trends and personal experiences navigating the complexities of career development, I've come to understand that these qualities are akin to a compass and map in the journey of modern employment. They guide us through uncharted territories and help us chart new paths when old ones become obsolete.

The Foundation of Resilience

Resilience is the bedrock upon which a sustainable career is built. It's the inner strength that allows us to rebound from setbacks, failures, and rejections, which are inevitable aspects of any career journey. Cultivating resilience begins with a mindset that views challenges as opportunities for growth and learning. It involves embracing a perspective that every experience, especially the difficult ones, adds a layer of depth and strength to our professional persona.

To build resilience, start by fostering a positive yet realistic outlook. Celebrate successes, however small, and view failures as feedback, not setbacks. Develop a support network of colleagues, mentors, and peers who can offer perspective, advice, and encouragement when the going gets tough. Remember, resilience is not about going it alone; it's about knowing when to seek support and how to use it to bounce back stronger.

Adaptability: The Art of Evolution

Adaptability is the ability to adjust to new conditions and environments swiftly and efficiently. In a job market characterized by rapid technological advancements and shifting economic landscapes, adaptability is what allows us to pivot, evolve, and embrace new opportunities that arise from change.

Enhancing adaptability involves staying curious and open-minded, constantly seeking to expand your knowledge base and skill set. It means being proactive about learning new technologies, methodologies, and industry trends. Embrace cross-disciplinary learning to diversify your skills and perspectives, making you more agile in the face of change.

Strategic Flexibility in Career Planning

Strategic flexibility is a higher-order dimension of adaptability. It involves not just reacting to change but anticipating it and planning accordingly. This requires a keen understanding of industry trends and foresight to predict how these trends could impact your career. Regularly assess your career path and goals, and be willing to make adjustments based on the evolving job market. This might mean pursuing additional training, rebranding yourself, or even changing career directions entirely.

Emotional Intelligence: The Adaptable Mind's Companion

Emotional intelligence (EI) plays a pivotal role in both resilience and adaptability. The ability to manage your emotions, empathize with others, and navigate social complexities aids in building strong professional relationships and creating a supportive network. EI also enhances decision-making and problem-solving under stress, critical components of navigating career challenges effectively.

Cultivating a Continuous Learning Mindset

At the core of adaptability lies a continuous learning mindset. This involves an ongoing commitment to personal and professional development, seeking out learning opportunities, and remaining open to new ideas and perspectives. It's about being a lifelong learner, recognizing that the end of one learning journey is simply the beginning of another.

Conclusion

In conclusion, cultivating resilience and adaptability is about more than just surviving in the modern job market; it's about thriving, growing, and finding fulfillment in the face of change. It requires a balanced approach of inner strength and outward flexibility, emotional intelligence, and a continuous commitment to learning and development. By fostering these qualities, we equip ourselves not just to navigate the challenges of today's employment landscape but to seize the opportunities it presents, crafting a career that is not only successful but also resilient, adaptable, and deeply rewarding.

Appendices

Resources for Job Seekers

In the labyrinthine journey of job searching and career development, having a compass in the form of reliable resources can make all the difference. Throughout my exploration of the employment landscape, I've encountered numerous tools, platforms, and communities that have been invaluable not just to me, but to countless others navigating similar paths. Here, I share a curated selection of these resources, each chosen for its proven value in enhancing job search strategies, skill development, networking opportunities, and more.

Online Job Boards and Platforms

- **LinkedIn**: Beyond a professional networking site, LinkedIn has evolved into a comprehensive job search platform, offering job listings, company insights, and the ability to connect directly with hiring managers and recruiters.

- **Indeed**: As one of the largest job search engines globally, Indeed aggregates listings from thousands of websites, offering an extensive range of opportunities across industries.

- **Glassdoor**: Known for its company reviews, Glassdoor also provides job listings and salary insights, enabling job seekers to make informed decisions about potential employers.

Skill Development and Learning

- **Coursera** and **edX**: These platforms offer courses from universities and colleges worldwide, covering a vast array of subjects and skills, from data science to business management.

- **Udemy**: With a focus on professional and personal development, Udemy features courses in various fields, including technology, design, and marketing, often taught by industry experts.

- **LinkedIn Learning**: Offering video courses taught by industry experts in software, creative, and business skills, LinkedIn Learning is a valuable resource for those looking to upskill or reskill.

Networking and Professional Development

- **Meetup**: This platform facilitates in-person and virtual gatherings of people with shared interests, including professional networking groups, tech meetups, and industry-specific seminars.

- **Professional Associations**: Joining industry-specific associations can provide access to exclusive job boards, networking events, and professional development resources.

- **Alumni Networks**: University alumni networks can be a goldmine for connections, mentorship opportunities, and industry insights.

Resume and Cover Letter Tools

- **Canva**: Known for its design templates, Canva offers a variety of professional resume templates that can help job seekers create visually appealing resumes.

- **Grammarly**: This writing assistant tool can be invaluable for proofreading and polishing resumes and cover letters, ensuring they are error-free and professionally presented.

Interview Preparation

- **Big Interview**: An online system that combines training and practice to help improve interview techniques and build confidence.

- **Pramp**: Offers peer-to-peer mock interviews for a variety of disciplines, allowing users to practice both sides of the interview process.

Freelancing and Gig Work Platforms

- **Upwork** and **Freelancer**: These platforms connect freelancers with businesses that need their skills. Opportunities range from writing and graphic design to web development and marketing.

- **Fiverr**: Emphasizes the selling of freelance services by showcasing your projects and letting clients come to you.

Remote Work Resources

- **We Work Remotely** and **Remote.co**: These websites list remote job opportunities across various fields, catering to the growing demand for flexible, location-independent work.

Mental Health and Well-being

- **Headspace** and **Calm**: Apps offering meditation and mindfulness practices, essential for maintaining mental health during the job search process.

- **Talkspace** and **BetterHelp**: Provide online therapy services, offering support for those dealing with job search stress or career transition anxiety.

Conclusion

This compendium of resources is designed to arm job seekers with the tools necessary to navigate the complexities of the modern job market. From honing in-demand skills to crafting standout resumes, preparing for interviews, and building a robust professional network, these resources offer a pathway to not just finding a job, but forging a meaningful and fulfilling career. Remember, the key to leveraging these tools effectively lies in a proactive approach, a willingness to learn, and the resilience to persevere through the challenges that inevitably arise on the journey to career success.

Glossary of Key Terms

In navigating the multifaceted landscape of today's job market, it's crucial to be fluent in the language that defines it. This glossary is designed to demystify key terms and concepts that recur throughout the journey of modern employment, providing clarity and enhancing understanding for job seekers and career changers alike.

- **Artificial Intelligence (AI)**: A branch of computer science dedicated to creating systems capable of performing tasks that typically require human intelligence, such as learning, decision-making, and language understanding. In the job market, AI is both a disruptor, automating certain tasks, and an enabler, creating new opportunities for human-AI collaboration.

- **Automation**: The use of technology to perform tasks without human intervention. In the workplace, automation can streamline operations, but it also necessitates the evolution of workforce skills to adapt to changing job roles.

- **Digital Footprint**: The trail of data you leave on the internet, including social media profiles, website comments, and more. In a job search, maintaining a professional digital footprint is crucial, as potential employers often review online profiles during the hiring process.

- **Gig Economy**: A labor market characterized by short-term contracts or freelance work as opposed to permanent jobs. It offers flexibility and variety, but also presents challenges in terms of job security and benefits.

- **Lifelong Learning**: The ongoing, voluntary, and self-motivated pursuit of knowledge for either personal or professional reasons. It's essential in today's rapidly changing job market, ensuring individuals remain competitive and adaptable.

- **Networking**: The process of interacting with others to exchange information and develop professional or social contacts. Effective networking can uncover hidden job opportunities and lead to career advancements.

- **Personal Branding**: The practice of marketing oneself and one's career as brands. It involves carefully curating one's online presence and offline interactions to align with career goals and values.

- **Remote Work**: A working style that allows professionals to work outside of a traditional office environment, often from home. It relies heavily on digital communication technologies.

- **Resilience**: The capacity to recover quickly from difficulties; toughness. In career development, resilience is about bouncing back from setbacks and persisting in the face of challenges.

- **Skill Set**: A combination of abilities, qualities, and experiences you can apply to perform tasks well. With the job market's constant evolution, adapting and expanding one's skill set is key to staying relevant.

- **Soft Skills**: Non-technical skills that relate to how you work and interact with others. They include interpersonal skills, communication skills, listening skills, time management, and empathy, among others.

- **Upskilling**: The process of learning new or improving existing skills to stay relevant in one's current role or industry. It's a crucial part of career development in an ever-evolving job market.

- **Work-Life Balance**: The equilibrium between professional life and personal life. A healthy work-life balance is essential for mental health and overall well-being.

- **Freelancing**: Offering your services on a project or task basis, usually as an independent contractor. It's a common practice in the gig economy, allowing for flexibility but requiring self-management and discipline.

By familiarizing yourself with these terms and integrating them into your career strategy, you can navigate the complexities of the modern job market with greater ease and confidence. This glossary is not exhaustive, but it provides a foundation for understanding the key concepts that are integral to the journey of contemporary job seekers and career builders.

Summary

108